Gift of Friendship

Edited by
Nick Beilenson

Illustrated by
Sandy Baenen and
Peter Chope

PETER PAUPER PRESS, INC.
WHITE PLAINS • NEW YORK

To *Mary Alice Warner*
Compilation copyright © 1987
Peter Pauper Press, Inc.
Flower Illustrations copyright © 1987
Dear Violet, Inc.,
Palo Alto, California
ISBN 0-88088-216-6
Library of Congress No. 86-63857
Printed in the United States of America

A COLLECTION OF
WARM, BEAUTIFUL
THOUGHTS ABOUT THE LOVE OF
ONE HEART FOR ANOTHER

Tulip

Gift of Friendship

Friends are like melons; shall I tell you why? To find one good you must a hundred try.

CLAUDE MERMET

Laughter is not a bad beginning for a friendship, and it is the best ending for one.

OSCAR WILDE

When friends ask there is no tomorrow.

PROVERB

"Stay" is a charming word in a friend's vocabulary.

AMOS BRONSON ALCOTT

5

To meet an old friend in a distant country is like the delight of rain after a long drought.

A real friend is one who walks in when the rest of the world walks out.

WALTER WINCHELL

The best way to keep friendships from breaking is not to drop them.

If you wish to know the character of the prince, look at his ministers; if you wish to understand the man, look at his friends; if you wish to know the father, observe his son.

Judge not thy friend until thou standest in his place.

RABBI HILLEL

Friendship often ends in love; but love, in friendship—never.

CHARLES CALEB COLTON

A friend you have to buy won't be worth what you pay for him.

G. D. PRENTICE

The greatest healing therapy is friendship and love.

HUBERT HUMPHREY

Elizabeth Barrett Browning: What is the secret of your life? Tell me, that I may make mine beautiful, too.
Charles Kingsley: I had a friend.

In prosperity our friends know us; in adversity we know our friends.

JOHN CHURTON COLLINS

Friendship is a plant of slow growth and must undergo and withstand the shocks of adversity before it is entitled to the appellation.

GEORGE WASHINGTON

What is a friend? A single soul dwelling in two bodies.

ARISTOTLE

I think this is the beginning of a beautiful friendship.

HUMPHREY BOGART
To Claude Rains in Casablanca

It is easy to dodge the arrow of an enemy, but difficult to avoid the spear of a friend. It is also easy to escape from the pitfall of suffering, but difficult to get out of the snare of pleasure.

CHINESE EPIGRAM

My coat and I live comfortably together. It has assumed all my wrinkles, does not hurt me anywhere, has moulded itself on my deformities, and is complacent to all my movements, and I only feel its presence because it keeps me warm. Old coats and old friends are the same thing.

VICTOR HUGO

It is better to be in chains with friends than in a garden with strangers.

PERSIAN PROVERB

Friendship is like a bank account: you cannot continue to draw on it without making deposits.

Instead of loving your enemies, treat your friends a little better.

EDGAR W. ("ED") HOWE

Love all, trust a few,
Do wrong to none: be able for thine enemy
Rather in power than use, and keep thy
  friend
Under thy own life's key: be checked for
  silence,
But never taxed for speech.

WILLIAM SHAKESPEARE
All's Well That Ends Well

Always forgive your enemies; nothing an-
noys them so much.

OSCAR WILDE

God never loved me in so sweet a way before.
'Tis He alone who can such blessings send.
And when His love would new expressions
  find,
He brought thee to me and He said—"Be-
  hold a friend.

ANONYMOUS

It is a mistake to think that one makes a friend because of his or her qualities; it has nothing to do with qualities at all. It is the person that we want, not what he does or says, or does not do or say, but what he *is* that is eternally enough! Who shall explain the extraordinary instinct that tells us, perhaps after a single meeting, that this or that particular person in some mysterious way matters to us? I confess that, for myself, I never enter a new company without the hope that I may discover a friend, perhaps *the* friend, sitting there with an expectant smile. That hope survives a thousand disappointments. People who deal with life generously and large-heartedly go on multiplying relationships to the end.

ARTHUR CHRISTOPHER BENSON

It is chance that makes brothers, but hearts that make friends.

ANONYMOUS

I love you not only for what you are, but for what I am when I am with you.

I love you not only for what you have made of yourself, but for what you are making of me.

I love you because you have done more than any creed could have done to make me good, and more than any fate could have done to make me happy.

You have done it without a touch, without a word, without a sign.

You have done it by being yourself. Perhaps that is what being a friend means, after all.

ANONYMOUS

The only rose without thorns is friendship.

MADELEINE DE SCUDERY

12

Rose

You can choose your friends but you can't choose your relatives.

CHARLIE BROWN

A friend in need is a friend indeed.

ENGLISH PROVERB

Histories are more full of examples of the fidelity of dogs than of friends.

ALEXANDER POPE

I want someone to laugh with me, someone to be grave with me, someone to please me and help my discrimination with his or her own remark, and at times, no doubt, to admire my acuteness and penetration.

ROBERT BURNS

Friendship is Love without his wings.

LORD BYRON

Chance makes our parents, but choice
makes our friends.

JACQUES DELILLE

The child alone is the true democrat; to
him only is every one he meets a friend.

ANONYMOUS

Friendship maketh daylight in the understanding, out of darkness and confusion of
thought.

FRANCIS BACON

Do not keep the alabaster boxes of your
love and tenderness sealed up until your
friends are dead. Fill their lives with sweetness. Speak approving cheering words
while their ears can hear them and while
their hearts can be thrilled by them.

HENRY WARD BEECHER

As gold more splendid from the fire appears;
Thus friendship brightens by the length
  of years.

THOMAS CARLYLE

True friends, like ivy and the wall
Both stand together, and together fall.

THOMAS CARLYLE

Friendship cannot live with Ceremony, nor
without Civility.

BENJAMIN FRANKLIN

One can do without people, but one has
need of a friend.

CHINESE WISDOM

Friendship is simply loving agreement in
all life's questions.

CICERO

I want a warm and faithful friend,
  To cheer the adverse hour;
Who ne'er to flatter will descend,
  Nor bend the knee to power,—
A friend to chide me when I'm wrong,
  My inmost soul to see;
And that my friendship prove as strong
  For him as his for me.

JOHN QUINCY ADAMS

If a man could mount to Heaven and survey the mighty universe, his admiration of its beauties would be much diminished unless he had someone to share in his pleasure.

CICERO

I find as I grow older that I love those most whom I loved first.

THOMAS JEFFERSON

In poverty and other misfortunes of life, true friends are a sure refuge. The young they keep out of mischief; to the old they are a comfort and aid in their weakness, and those in the prime of life they incite to noble deeds.

ARISTOTLE

Be slow in choosing a friend, slower in changing.

BENJAMIN FRANKLIN

Friendship hath the skill and observation of the best physician, the diligence and vigilance of the best nurse, and the tenderness and patience of the best mother.

EDWARD CLARENDON

To accept a favor from a friend is to confer one.

JOHN CHURTON COLLINS

Neither a borrower, nor a lender be;
For loan oft loses both itself and friend,
And borrowing dulls the edge of
    husbandry
This above all: to thine own self be true,
And it must follow, as the night the day,
Thou canst not then be false to any man.

WILLIAM SHAKESPEARE

True friendship is like sound health, the
value of it is seldom known until it be lost.

CHARLES CALEB COLTON

Hast thou a friend? Thou has indeed
    A rich and large supply,
Treasure to serve your every need,
    Well managed, till you die.

WILLIAM COWPER

To love someone means to see him as God
intended him.

FYODOR DOSTOYEVSKY

If thou findest a good man, rise up early in the morning to go to him, and let thy feet wear the steps of his door.

ECCLESIASTICUS

What do we live for, if it is not to make life less difficult to others?

GEORGE ELIOT

The glory of friendship is not the out-stretched hand, nor the kindly smile, nor the joy of companionship; it is the spiritual inspiration that comes to one when he discovers that someone else believes in him and is willing to trust him with his friendship.

RALPH WALDO EMERSON

A day for toil, an hour for sport,
But for a friend is life too short.

RALPH WALDO EMERSON

The ornament of a house is the friends
who frequent it.
RALPH WALDO EMERSON

God evidently does not intend us all to be
rich, or powerful or great, but He does intend us all to be friends.
RALPH WALDO EMERSON

Nothing more dangerous than a friend
without discretion; even a prudent enemy
is preferable.
JEAN DE LA FONTAINE

A Father's a Treasure; a Brother's a Comfort; a Friend is both.
BENJAMIN FRANKLIN

Little friends may prove great friends.
AESOP

A brother may not be a friend, but a friend will always be a brother.

BENJAMIN FRANKLIN

They only are true friends who think as one.

FRENCH PROVERB

There is no better looking-glass than an old friend.

THOMAS FULLER

There are three faithful friends—an old wife, an old dog, and ready money.

BENJAMIN FRANKLIN

If at first you don't succeed, you'll probably have more friends.

For believe me, in this world, which is ever slipping from under our feet, it is the prerogative of friendship to grow old with one's friends.

ARTHUR S. HARDY

We never know the true value of friends. While they live we are too sensitive of their faults: when we have lost them we only see their virtues.

J. C. AND A. W. HARE

To be capable of steady friendship and lasting love, are the two greatest proofs, not only of goodness of heart, but of strength of mind.

WILLIAM HAZLITT

A friendless man is like a left hand without a right.

HEBREW PROVERB

Camelia

Tell me with whom thou art found and I will tell thee who thou art.

JOHANN WOLFGANG VON GOETHE

It is great to have friends when one is young, but indeed it is still more so when one is getting old. When one is young, friends are, like everything else, a matter of course. In the older years one knows what it means to have them.

EDVARD GRIEG

To friendship every burden's light.

JOHN GAY

Love is a sudden blaze, which soon decays;
Friendship is like the sun's eternal rays;
Not daily benefits exhaust the flame;
It still is giving, and still burns the same.

JOHN GAY

Here's a bottle and an honest friend!
  What wad ye wish for mair, man?
Wha kens, before his life may end,
  What his share may be o' care, man?
Then catch the moments as they fly,
  And use them as ye ought, man:—
Believe me, happiness is shy,
  And comes not aye when sought, man.
                                ROBERT BURNS

One friend in a lifetime is much; two are
many; three are hardly possible. Friendship
needs a certain parallelism of life, a com-
munity of thought, a rivalry of aim.
                                HENRY ADAMS

To keep friends, treat them kindly; to kill
friends, treat them often.

All men's friend, no man's friend.
                                JOHN WODROEPHE

A true friend laughs at your stories even when they're not so good, and sympathizes with your troubles even when they're not so bad.

Every true friend is a glimpse of God.

LUCY LARCOM

I desire so to conduct the affairs of this administration that if at the end, when I come to lay down the reins of power, I have lost every other friend on earth, I shall at least have one friend left, and that friend shall be down inside of me.

ABRAHAM LINCOLN

When two friends part they should lock up each other's secrets and exchange keys. The truly noble mind has no resentments.

DIOGENES

I never considered a difference of opinion
in politics, in religion, in philosophy, as
cause for withdrawing from a friend.

THOMAS JEFFERSON

Each year to ancient friendships adds a
    ring
As to an oak.

JAMES RUSSELL LOWELL

Every one must have felt that a cheerful
friend is like a sunny day, which sheds its
brightness on all around; and most of us
can, as we choose, make of this world a
palace or a prison.

SIR JOHN LUBBOCK

When adversities flow, then love ebbs; but
friendship standeth stiffly in storms.

JOHN LYLY

Communion with the good is friendship's
root,
   That dieth not until our death;
And on the boughs hang ever golden
fruit:—
   And this is friendship, the world saith.

Ourselves we doubt, our hearts we hardly
know,
   We lean for guidance on a friend;
Ay, on a righteous man we'd fain bestow
   Our faith, and follow to the end.
                THE SANSKRIT OF BHARTRIHARI

To bury a friendship is a keener grief than
to bury a friend.
                        HUGH BLACK

The bird a nest, the spider a web, man
friendship.
                        WILLIAM BLAKE

Treat a friend as a person who may someday become your enemy; an enemy as a
person who may someday become your
friend.

GEORGE BERNARD SHAW

Friendship is an education. It draws the
friend out of himself and all that is selfish
and ignoble in him and leads him to life's
higher levels of altruism and sacrifice.
Many a man has been saved from a life of
frivolity and emptiness to a career of noble
service by finding at a critical hour the
right kind of friend.

G. D. PRENTICE

A faithful friend is a strong defense; and he
that hath found such a one hath found a
treasure. Nothing doth countervail a faithful friend, and his excellency is invaluable.

PROVERBS

Prosperity is no just scale; adversity is the only balance to weigh friends.

PLUTARCH

People who have warm friends are healthier and happier than those who have none. A single real friend is a treasure worth more than gold or precious stones. Money can buy many things, good and evil. All the wealth of the world could not buy you a friend or pay you for the loss of one.

G. D. PRENTICE

Love Him, and keep Him for thy Friend, who, when all go away, will not forsake thee, nor suffer thee to perish at the last.

THOMAS A KEMPIS

Friendship is like money, easier made than kept.

SAMUEL BUTLER

Friendship increases by visiting Friends,
but by visiting seldom.

BENJAMIN FRANKLIN

We learn our virtues from the friends who
love us; our faults from the enemy who
hates us. We cannot easily discover our
real character from a friend. He is a mirror, on which the warmth of our breath
impedes the clearness of the reflection.

JOHANN PAUL FRIEDRICH RICHTER

A little peaceful home
Bounds all my wants and wishes; add to this
My book and friend, and this is happiness.

FRANCESCO DI RIOJA

When my friends are one-eyed, I look at
their profile.

JOSEPH JOUBERT

Daffodil

It is a good and safe rule to sojourn in every place as if you meant to spend your life there, never omitting an opportunity of doing a kindness, or speaking a true word, or making a friend.

JOHN RUSKIN

The love of friendship should be gratuitous. You ought not to have or to love a friend for what he will give you. If you love him for the reason that he will supply you with money or some other temporal favor, you love the gift rather than him. A friend should be loved freely for himself, and not for anything else.

ST. AUGUSTINE

Friendship is everything. Friendship is more than talent. It is more than government. It is almost the equal of family.

FROM THE GODFATHER

Friends are needed both for joy and for sorrow.

YIDDISH PROVERB

The mind is rarely so disturbed, but that the company of a friend will restore it to some degree of tranquility and sedateness.

ADAM SMITH

Frank explanations with friends in case of affronts sometimes save a perishing friendship; sometimes they even place it on a firmer basis than before. Secret discontent always ends badly. And by the way, we ought to remember that the word *friendship* applies to relationships in the family quite as much as with outsiders. Somebody once said that love may not be any part of friendship but friendship must always exist for love to be happy.

SYDNEY SMITH

Many kinds of fruit grow upon the tree of life, but none so sweet as friendship; as with the orange tree its blossoms and fruit appear at the same time, full of refreshment for sense and for soul.

LUCY LARCOM

In the hour of distress and misery the eye of every mortal turns to friendship; in the hour of gladness and conviviality, what is our want? It is friendship. When the heart overflows with gratitude, or with any other sweet and sacred sentiment, what is the word to which it would give utterance? A friend.

WALTER SAVAGE LANDOR

Good words shall gain you honor in the market-place; but good deeds shall gain you friends among men.

LAO-TSE

Friendship improves happiness, and abates misery, by doubling our joy, and dividing our grief.

JOSEPH ADDISON

One of the most beautiful qualities of true friendship is to understand and to be understood.

SENECA

The comfort of having a friend may be taken away, but not that of having had one.

SENECA

I count myself in nothing else so happy
As in a soul remembering my good friends.

WILLIAM SHAKESPEARE

The best mirror is an old friend.

GEORGE HERBERT

Old friends are best. King James used to
call for his old shoes; they were easiest for
his feet.

JOHN SELDEN

The language of friendship is not words,
but meanings. It is an intelligence above
language.

HENRY DAVID THOREAU

The proper office of a friend is to side with
you when you are in the wrong. Nearly
anybody will side with you when you are
in the right.

MARK TWAIN

One who looks for a friend without faults
will have none.

HASIDIC SAYING

The true test of friendship is to be able to sit or walk with a friend for an hour in perfect silence without wearying of one another's company.

DINAH MARIA MULOCK CRAIK

I choose my friends for their good looks, my acquaintances for their characters, and my enemies for their brains.

OSCAR WILDE

Woe to him whom nobody likes, but beware of him whom everybody likes.

HASIDIC SAYING

Friendship can be purchased only by friendship. A man may have authority over others, but he can never have their heart but by giving his own.

THOMAS WILSON

Marriage is like a three-speed gearbox: affection, friendship, love. It is not advisable to crash your gears and go right through to love straightaway. You need to ease your way through. The basis of love is respect, and that needs to be learned from affection and friendship.

PETER USTINOV

Friends must frankly and sharply admonish each other, and brothers must be gentle toward one another.

CONFUCIUS

With every friend I love who has been taken into the brown bosom of the earth a part of me has been buried there; but their contribution to my being of happiness, strength and understanding remains to sustain me in an altered world.

HELEN KELLER

Iris

A friendship will be young after the lapse of half a century; a passion is old at the end of three months.

MADAME SWETCHINE

A witty comrade at your side,
To walk's as easy as to ride.

PUBLILIUS SYRUS

'Tis great Confidence in a Friend to tell him your Faults, greater to tell him his.

BENJAMIN FRANKLIN

A Friend is one who incessantly pays us the compliment of expecting from us all the virtues, and who can appreciate them in us.

Go often to the house of thy friend for weeds choke up the unused path.

It takes your enemy and your friend,
working together, to hurt you to the heart;
the one to slander you and the other to get
the news to you.

MARK TWAIN

You can choose your friends, but you only
have one mother.

MAX SHULMAN

It is better to decide an argument between
enemies than friends; for one friend will
certainly become an enemy and one enemy
a friend.

The only man who behaves sensibly is my
tailor; he takes my measure anew every
time he sees me, whilst all the rest go on
with their old measurements, and expect
them to fit me.

GEORGE BERNARD SHAW

Promises may get friends, but 'tis performance that keeps them.

Do good to thy friend to keep him, to thy enemy to gain him.

BENJAMIN FRANKLIN

Friendship is constant in all other things
Save in the office and affairs of love:
Therefore all hearts in love use their own
    tongues;
Let every eye negotiate for itself
And trust no agent.

WILLIAM SHAKESPEARE

A friend who cannot at a pinch remember
a thing or two that never happened is as
bad as one who does not know how to forget.

SAMUEL BUTLER

"A drop of honey catches more flies than a gallon of gall." So with men. If you would win a man to your cause, first convince him that you are his sincere friend. Therein is a drop of honey which catches his heart, which, say what he will, is the highroad to his reason . . .

ABRAHAM LINCOLN

He who throws away a friend is as bad as he who throws away his life.

SOPHOCLES

Few people give themselves time to be friends.

ROBERT SOUTHEY

We are all travellers in the wilderness of this world, and the best that we find in our travels is an honest friend.

ROBERT LOUIS STEVENSON

Promises may get thee friends, but non-performance will turn them into enemies.

Sorrow is like a precious treasure, shown only to friends.

PROVERB FROM MADAGASCAR

A false friend and a shadow attend only while the sun shines.

He is my friend that helps me, and not he that pities me.

You cannot joke an enemy into a friend, but you may joke a friend into an enemy.

To be without a friend, is to be poor, indeed.

PROVERB FROM SOMALIA

Anybody can sympathize with the sufferings of a friend, but it requires a very fine nature to sympathize with a friend's success.

OSCAR WILDE

Never speak ill of yourself; your friends will always say enough on that subject.

CHARLES M. DE TALLEYRAND-PÉRIGORD

I like a friend the better for having faults that one can talk about.

WILLIAM HAZLITT

An open Foe may prove a curse;
But a pretended Friend is worse.

BENJAMIN FRANKLIN

Better lose a jest than a friend.

Violet

I shot an arrow into the air,
It fell to earth, I know not where;
For, so swiftly it flew, the sight
Could not follow it in its flight.

I breathed a song into the air,
It fell to earth, I knew not where;
For who has sight so keen and strong,
That it can follow the flight of song?

Long, long afterward, in an oak
I found the arrow, still unbroke;
And the song, from beginning to end,
I found again in the heart of a friend.

HENRY WADSWORTH LONGFELLOW
The Arrow and the Song

Friendship cheers like a sunbeam; charms
like a good story; inspires like a brave lead-
er; binds like a golden chain; guides like a
heavenly vision.

NEWELL D. HILLIS

Real friends are people who let you have your own truths.

Reprove your friends in secret, praise them openly.

PUBLILIUS SYRUS

Greater love hath no man than this, that a man lay down his life for his friends.

NEW TESTAMENT: JOHN 15:13

A man, Sir, should keep his friendships in constant repair.

SAMUEL JOHNSON

The feeling of friendship is like that of being comfortably filled with roast beef; love, like being enlivened with champagne.

SAMUEL JOHNSON

Despite the bitterness engendered by the Civil War, Lincoln never missed an opportunity to speak kindly of the South. An ardent Union supporter once took him to task for this attitude. "Why try to make friends with your enemies?" he protested. "You should destroy them."

"Am I not destroying my enemies," gently replied Lincoln, "when I make friends of them?"

A friendship founded on business is a good deal better than a business founded on friendship.

JOHN D. ROCKEFELLER

You can make more friends in two months by becoming interested in other people than you can in two years by trying to get other people interested in you.

DALE CARNEGIE

There is no friend like an old friend
   Who has shared our morning days,
No greeting like his welcome,
   No homage like his praise.

OLIVER WENDELL HOLMES

Choose thy friends like thy books, few but choice.

JAMES HOWELL

Alonso of Aragon was wont to say in commendation of age, that age appears to be best in four things—old wood best to burn, old wine to drink, old friends to trust, and old authors to read.

FRANCIS BACON

The ideal of friendship is to feel as one while remaining two.

MADAME SWETCHINE

Be slow to fall into friendship; but when
thou art in, continue firm and constant.

SOCRATES

Ointment and perfume rejoice the heart; so
doth the sweetness of a man's friend that
cometh of hearty counsel.

SOLOMON

Blessed is the man that beholdeth the face of
    a friend in a far country,
The darkness of his heart is melted in the
    dawning of day within him,
It is like the sound of sweet music heard
long
    ago and half forgotten;
It is like the coming back of birds to a
wood
    where the winter is ended.

HENRY VAN DYKE

The friends of our friends are our friends.

PROVERB FROM ZAIRE

Thy friend has a friend, and thy friend's
friend has a friend: be discreet.

TALMUD

A visitor to the White House once asked
President Lincoln, "What is your definition
of a friend?" "My definition of a friend?"
the Great Emancipator repeated slowly:
"One who has the same enemies you
have."

To be intimate with a foolish friend, is like
going to bed to a razor.

Short accounts make long friends.

BALZAC

We need someone to believe in us—if we do well, we want our work commended, our faith corroborated. The individual who thinks well of you, who keeps his mind on your good qualities, and does not look for flaws, is your friend. Who is my brother? I'll tell you: he is one who recognizes the good in me.

ELBERT HUBBARD

Man has three friends on whose company he relies. First, wealth; which goes with him only while good fortune lasts. Second, his relatives; they go only as far as the grave, leave him there. The third friend, his good deeds, go with him beyond the grave.

TALMUD

When we lose a friend we die a little.

I find friendship to be like wine, raw when new, ripened with age, the true old man's milk and restorative cordial.

THOMAS JEFFERSON

So long as we love, we serve. So long as we are loved by others we are indispensable; and no man is useless while he has a friend.

ROBERT LOUIS STEVENSON

Thy friendship oft has made my heart to
  ache:
Do be my enemy—for friendship's sake.

WILLIAM BLAKE

Trouble is a great sieve through which we sift our acquaintances; those who are too big to pass through are friends.

NORTH CAROLINA CHURCHMAN

What is a Friend? I'll tell you. It is a person with whom you dare to be yourself. Your soul can go naked with him. He seems to ask you to put on nothing, only to be what you really are.

When you are with him, you do not have to be on your guard. You can say what you think, so long as it is genuinely you.

He understands those contradictions in your nature that cause others to misjudge you. With him you breathe freely—you can avow your little vanities and envies and absurdities, and in opening them up to him they are dissolved on the white ocean of his loyalty.

He understands.—You can weep with him, laugh with him, pray with him— through and underneath it all he sees, knows and loves you.

ANONYMOUS

A slender acquaintance with the world must convince every man that actions, not words, are the true criterion of the attachment of friends; and that the most liberal professions of good-will are very far from being the surest marks of it.

GEORGE WASHINGTON

When a man on light grounds breaks off his friendship with the poor and mean, and only on great grounds with the rich and noble, his love of worth cannot be great, nor does his hatred of evil greatly appear. Though others may say that he is not influenced by love of gain, I do not believe them.

CONFUCIUS

I love such mirth as does not make friends ashamed to look upon one another next morning.

As widowers proverbially marry again, so a man with the habit of friendship always finds new friends. . . . My old age judges more charitably and thinks better of mankind than my youth ever did. I discount idealization, I forgive onesidedness, I see that it is essential to perfection of any kind. And in each person I catch the fleeting suggestion of something beautiful, and swear eternal friendship with that.

GEORGE SANTAYANA

Friendship is the inexpressible comfort of feeling safe with a person having neither to weigh thoughts nor measure words.

GEORGE ELIOT

Friendship above all ties does bind the
    heart,
And faith in friendship is the noblest part.

LORD ORRERY

Friends are the ancient and honorable of the earth. The oldest men did not begin friendship. It is older than Hindustan and the Chinese Empire. How long it has been cultivated, and still it is the staple article! It is a divine league forever struck.

HENRY DAVID THOREAU

We make more enemies by what we say than friends by what we do.

JOHN CHURTON COLLINS

A man's love is the measure of his fitness for good or bad company here or elsewhere. Men are tattooed with their special beliefs like so many South Sea Islanders; but a real human heart with divine love in it, beats with the same glow under all patterns of all earth's thousand tribes.

OLIVER WENDELL HOLMES

Friends! in this world of hurry
    And work and sudden end—
If a thought comes quick of doing
    A kindness to a friend—
Do it this very instant!
    Don't put it off—don't wait!
What's the use of doing a kindness
    If you do it a day too late?

CHARLES KINGSLEY

There is no word in the Latin language
that signifies a female friend. *Amica* means
a mistress: and perhaps there is no friendship betwixt the sexes wholly disunited
from a degree of love.

WILLIAM SHENSTONE

After friendship it is confidence; before
friendship it is judgment.

SENECA

Friendship is the pleasing game of inter-
changing praise.

OLIVER WENDELL HOLMES

Time draweth wrinkles in a fair face, but
addeth fresh colors to a fast friend, which
neither heat, nor cold, nor misery, nor
place, nor destiny, can alter or diminish.

JOHN LYLY

If instead of a gem, or even a flower, we
should cast the gift of rich thought into the
heart of a friend, that would be giving as
the angels give.

GEORGE MACDONALD

A crowd is not a company, and faces are
but a gallery of pictures, and talk but a tink-
ling cymbal, where there is no love.

FRANCIS BACON

But, after all, the very best thing in good talk, and the thing that helps most, is friendship. How it dissolves the barriers that divide us, and loosens all constraint, and diffuses itself like some fine old cordial through all the veins of life—this feeling that we understand and trust each other, and wish each other heartily well! Everything into which it really comes is good.

HENRY VAN DYKE

Of all felicities, the most charming is that of a firm and gentle friendship. It sweetens all our cares, dispels our sorrows, and counsels us in all extremities. Nay, if there were no other comfort in it than the bare exercise of so generous a virtue, even for that single reason a man would not be without it; it is a sovereign antidote against all calamities—even against the fear of death itself.

SENECA

Madam, I have been looking for a person who disliked gravy all my life; let us swear eternal friendship.

SYDNEY SMITH

Every man should have a fair sized cemetery in which to bury the faults of his friends.

HENRY BROOKS ADAMS

Friendship is the hardest thing in the world to explain. It's not something you learn in school. But if you haven't learned the meaning of friendship, you really haven't learned anything.

MUHAMMAD ALI

Friendship is the only cement that will ever hold the world together.

WOODROW WILSON